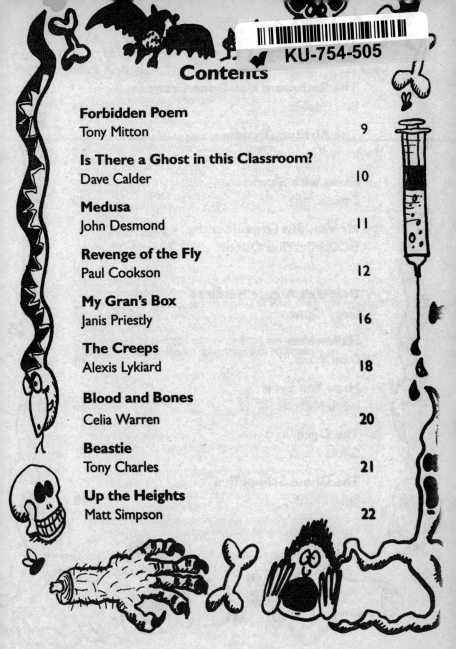

KU-754-505

Contents

The Ghoul School Bus

David Orme lives in Winchester and is the author of a wide range of poetry books, textbooks and picture books for children. When he is not writing he visits schools, performing poetry, running poetry workshops and encouraging children and teachers to enjoy poetry.

Also by Macmillan

'ERE WE GO!
Football Poems chosen by David Orme

THE SECRET LIVES OF TEACHERS
Revealing Rhymes chosen by Brian Moses

CUSTARD PIE
Poems that are Jokes that are Poems chosen by
Pie Corbett

TONGUE TWISTERS AND TONSIL TWIZZLERS
A Tantalising Tangle of Poems chosen by
Paul Cookson

NOTHING TASTES QUITE LIKE A GERBIL
and Other Vile Verses chosen by Brian Moses

ALIENS STOLE MY UNDERPANTS
and Other Intergalactic Poems chosen by
Brian Moses

SCHOOL TRIPS
Poems let loose by Brian Moses

THE GHOUL SCHOOL BUS

AND OTHER PETRIFYING POEMS

CHOSEN BY

DAVID ORME

Illustrated by David Woodward

**MACMILLAN
CHILDREN'S BOOKS**

First published 1994 by Macmillan Children's Books as
"Dracula's Auntie Ruthless"

This edition published 2000 by Macmillan Children's Books
a division of Macmillan Publishers Limited
25 Eccleston Place, London SW1W 9NF
Basingstoke and Oxford
Associated companies throughout the world
www.macmillan.com

ISBN 0 330 37524 5

Typeset by SX Composing DTP, Rayleigh, Essex
Printed and bound in Great Britain by Mackays of Chatham plc, Kent

Up the Heights from *The Pig's Thermal Underwear* (1993) reproduced by
permission of the author and Headland Productions.

Have You Ever? from *Higgledy-Humbug* (1990) reproduced by permission of
the author and Mary Glasgow Publications.

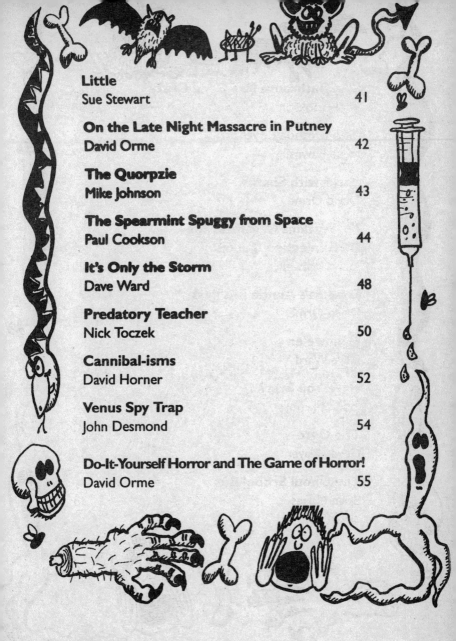

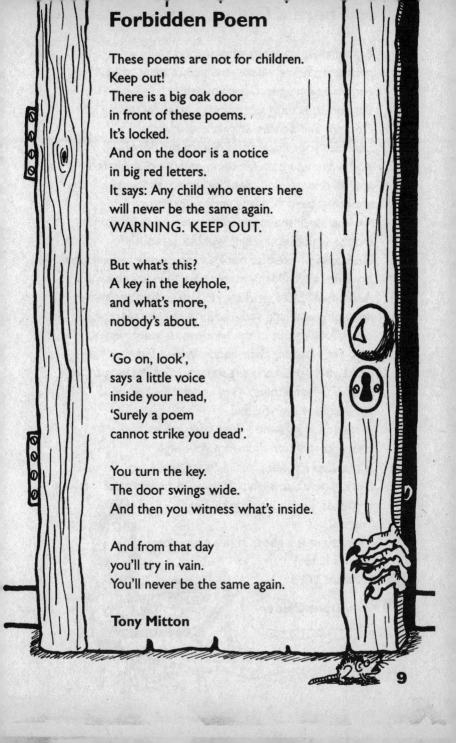

Forbidden Poem

These poems are not for children.
Keep out!
There is a big oak door
in front of these poems.
It's locked.
And on the door is a notice
in big red letters.
It says: Any child who enters here
will never be the same again.
WARNING. KEEP OUT.

But what's this?
A key in the keyhole,
and what's more,
nobody's about.

'Go on, look',
says a little voice
inside your head,
'Surely a poem
cannot strike you dead'.

You turn the key.
The door swings wide.
And then you witness what's inside.

And from that day
you'll try in vain.
You'll never be the same again.

Tony Mitton

Is There a Ghost in this Classroom?

Before anything, don't turn around,
ghosts are never where you expect them to be.
Let's look for signs. Does your desk lid
slam unexpectedly while you're carefully closing it?
Do pens and pencils wriggle and squirm,
slip from your fingers and dive to the floor?
And when you look for them, they've disappeared
and no one can find them for weeks and weeks
until they turn up dusty, under a radiator,
looking much the same but not feeling quite right?
Do the legs of your chair wobble nervously?
Do stacks of exercise books mysteriously slither apart
or your biro suddenly start to write in invisible ink?
And when you're working, do you sometimes sense
someone watching you – and it's not the teacher,
who's looking out of the window, or your friends,
who are watching their hands write – but
somewhere you can't see, but can feel like heat or light,
you know something's eyes are staring into you?
Now tell me, do you feel
A sudden small wind licking your ankles,
a slow cold shiver sliding up your leg?
Is there an icy itch prickling your neck?
Do you hear a soft whispering, so close and quiet
it sounds like it's inside your head?
You do?
Then there is a ghost in this classroom
and it's here
to haunt YOU.

Dave Calder

Medusa

Her hairstyle was original,
to say the least;
waving in the breeze it had
a life of it's own.
Her gaze held one's attention;
those who caught her eye
never left her side.
'Stone me!' They would murmur
and she did.

John Desmond

Revenge of the Fly

One day while eating breakfast,
bacon, ham and eggs,
a little fly buzzed down upon
the top of Billy's head.
It's little furry feet tickled
across young Billy's brow
and then it flew away
and he thought, 'It's okay now.'
He cut a piece of bacon,
looking forward to its taste,
was just about to munch it up
and then, across his face
he felt a little tickle
as the fly came in to land . . .
the bacon was uneaten
as the fork fell from his hand.
He shook his head and waved his arms
up, down and side to side
but the little fly just held on tight
no matter what he tried.

Just then the little fly buzzed off
and Billy with an evil grin said
'For sure that little monster's dead
when it comes back again.'
He found a rolled-up newspaper,
a tea towel and a shoe.
He lay in wait, his breakfast bait
and knew what he would do.
He heard a little buzzing noise
and then he heard it stop.
Creeping out then with a shout
he let the towel drop.
Armed with the shoe and paper
the fly beneath the towel
would not, could not escape.
He brought the paper flying down
with a squelchy, soggy SPLAT!
With an evil laugh he said
'Take that! And that! And that!'
The shoe crashed down until the plate
was smashed to smithereens
and a sticky, lumpy, splodgy mess
was all that could be seen.
Billy heard no buzzing now
but he heard his mum come in
so picking up the evidence
he threw it in the bin.

But, that night as Billy slept,
his window open wide
ten thousand million million flies
buzzed silently inside . . .
they hovered in the deadly swarm
above young Billy's bed
and with a shout of 'Tally Ho!'
they flew right at his head!
Up his nose, inside his ears,
across his sleeping eyes,
on his tongue and down his throat
They blocked up his insides.
No one heard him shout.
No one heard him cry
so just remember that
next time you kill a fly.
And if, by chance, you do kill one
then when you go to bed
make sure you close all windows
and cover up your head . . .

Paul Cookson

My Gran's Box

My gran collected wooden boxes.
That big one out there in the hall,
The one we all used to sit on,
It's a coffin, shroud, corpse and all.

Her pa brought it home from abroad.
He'd followed the custom out there,
And had Great-gran embalmed
As soon as she stopped breathing air.

Of course, she should have been buried,
But if he'd put her deep down in the ground,
She promised to come back and haunt him
So that's why her coffin's around.

Hey! Don't run away. Do stay with me,
My gran's this world's greatest cook.
We'll play some games, and eat our tea
Then we'll open the box so you can look!

Janis Priestley

The Creeps

The dream you often dream turns nightmare:
huge hurtling car out of control.
You're drowning slowly in quicksand.
Snakes slither by to chill the soul,

The parachute that will not open.
A suddenly unlocked, creaking door.
You're certain those loud footsteps quicken:
they're following you – they weren't, before.

A zombie shuffles down the hallway,
horribly hobbling, heavy and slow,
scaring you always into panic.
Should you hide? He'll find you! Where to go?

Stuck in a lift (who could have jammed it?)
thirty flights up. So do you dare
start climbing out into the blackness
or yell for help? There's no one there!

A vampire flaps at the gaping window,
silk cape as bloodshot as his eyes.
White fangs are flashing, he must bite you
but you can't budge, numbed by surprise.

Run through the graveyard: something's moving,
shrouded in grey among the tombs.
It seems to float, it can't be human:
in front of you the monster looms.

The best way of escaping horror,
pinching yourself till you're wide awake,
will always work – except for this time.
'Oh no!' a voice screams, 'there's some mistake!'

Alexis Lykiard

Blood and Bones

Under the floorboards, cold and deep,
Pipes are laid that drip and seep.
Down below the house, in the damp, dark mud,
Do they drip water or do they drip . . . ?

Blood in my arteries!
Blood in my veins!
I dreamt that blood ran
    down the drains!

High above the ceilings rafters creak.
Blind bats blunder. Mad mice squeak.
Up in the roof there are rattles and moans.
Is it the wind or chains and . . . ?

Bones in my body!
Bones in my head!
I dreamt there was a skeleton
    in my bed!

Celia Warren

Beastie

I rise at midnight from the black swamp
Beyond the city, where gaunt trees scrape at the sky.
I find my way by smell. A dog barks as I pass:
I put him to silence. Your garden walls
Are no barrier to me; I enter as I please.
In through cracks between bricks I slide,
Into the kitchen, where I make my preparations.
Nobody hears me as I climb the stairs.

Tony Charles

Up the Heights

living up the high-rise
eighteenth floor
lift never working
lighting poor

thousand concrete steps up
coming in from play
never know who you'll meet
coming the other way

in bed at night
things you hear
next door screeching
can hear them clear

shooting – must be telly! –
bang-bang-you're-dead!
who's playing drums now
above my head?

other side's toilet
listen to it flush
the cistern filling up again
with a terrible gush

who's that in the bath now
singing classy
I Did It My Way
Shirley Bassey?

adverts must be on now
whistling kettle
clink of cups and saucers
hope they're going to settle

O no!
howls and screams and gurgles!
won't sleep now old son
someone's put the Late Night
Horror Movie on!

Matt Simpson

The Bathroom Has Gone Crazy

The bathroom has gone crazy far beyond belief.
The sink is full of spiders and the toilet seat has teeth!

The plughole in the bath has a whirlpool underneath
that pulls you down feet first and the toilet seat has teeth!

The toothpaste tube is purple and makes your teeth fall out.
The toilet roll is nettles and makes you scream and shout!

The towels have got bristles, the bubble bath is glue,
the soap has turned to jelly and it makes your skin bright blue!

The mirror's pulling faces at everyone it can.
The shower's dripping marmalade and blackcurrant jam.

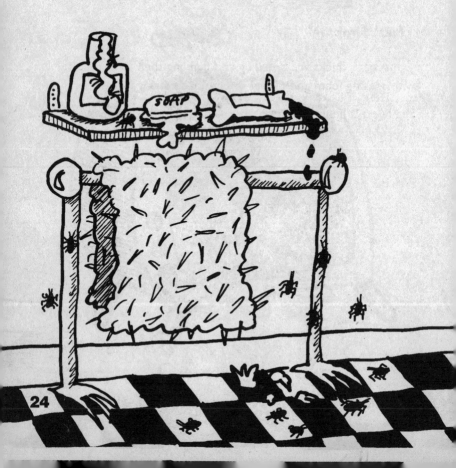

The rubber ducks are breeding and building their own nest
with shaving foam and tissues in Grandad's stringy vest.

Shampoo is liquid dynamite, there's petrol in the hairspray,
both will cure dandruff when they blow your head away!

The bathroom has gone crazy far beyond belief.
The sink is full of spiders and the toilet seat has teeth!

25

The toilet seat has teeth! Ow!
The toilet seat has teeth! Ow!
The toilet seat has teeth! Ow!
The toilet seat has teeth! Ow!

Crunch! Slurp! Munch! Burp!
The toilet seat has teeth! Ow!
Don't – sit – on – it!
The toilet seat has . . . ! Owwwww!

Paul Cookson

The Birthday Python

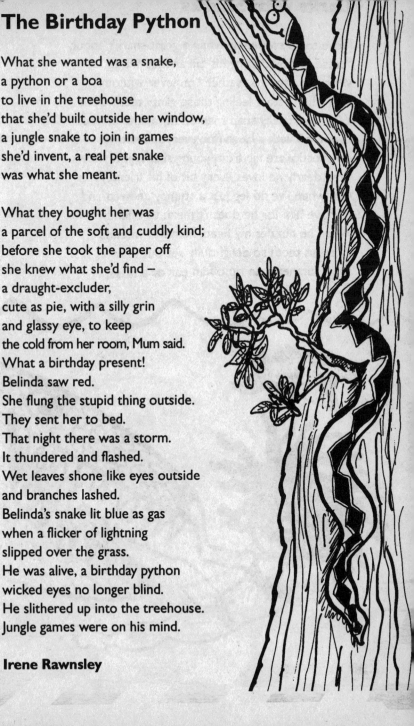

What she wanted was a snake,
a python or a boa
to live in the treehouse
that she'd built outside her window,
a jungle snake to join in games
she'd invent, a real pet snake
was what she meant.

What they bought her was
a parcel of the soft and cuddly kind;
before she took the paper off
she knew what she'd find –
a draught-excluder,
cute as pie, with a silly grin
and glassy eye, to keep
the cold from her room, Mum said.
What a birthday present!
Belinda saw red.
She flung the stupid thing outside.
They sent her to bed.
That night there was a storm.
It thundered and flashed.
Wet leaves shone like eyes outside
and branches lashed.
Belinda's snake lit blue as gas
when a flicker of lightning
slipped over the grass.
He was alive, a birthday python
wicked eyes no longer blind.
He slithered up into the treehouse.
Jungle games were on his mind.

Irene Rawnsley

Larks with Sharks

I love to go swimming when a great shark's about,
I tease him by tickling his tail and his snout
With the ostrich's feather I'm never without
And when I start feeling those glinty teeth close
With a scrunchy snap snap on my ankles or toes
I swim off with a laugh (for everyone knows
An affectionate nip from young sharky just shows
How dearly he loves every bit of his friend,)
And when I've no leg just a stumpy chewed end
I forgive him for he doesn't mean to offend;
When he nuzzles my head, he never intends
With his teeth so delightfully set out in rows
To go further than rip off an ear or a nose,

But when a shark's feeling playful, why, anything goes!
With tears in his eyes he'll take hold of my arm
Then twist himself round with such grace and such charm
The bits slip down his throat – no need for alarm!
I've another arm left! He means me no harm!

He'll play stretch and snap with six yards of insides
The rest will wash up on the beach with the tides
What fun we've all had, what a day to remember –
Yes, a shark loves a pal he can slowly dismember.

David Orme

Mr Watkins Organizes the BCG Injection Queue

Stop talking.
Stop trembling.
One straight line.
Heroes at the front.
Cowards at the back.

There is nothing to worry about.
Nothing.
Apart from the needle.

Forget the stories you've been told
About the pain.
It only hurts about as much as
Being run over.

And besides
Once the first five inches of needle
Have punctured your flesh
Most people
Pass out.

There is very little
Blood. Barely a
Bucketful.

And, of course, it's safe.
Last year we only had
Two fatalities.
So,
Most of you will live
Long enough to do your homework.

John Coldwell

Dracula's Auntie Ruthless

You've heard of old Drac
He's the one with the teeth
And a crumbly castle
With his tomb underneath.

Now he's bad enough
But you really just can't
Imagine the horror
That is Dracula's Aunt.

Even werewolves avoid her
Won't have her to stay
They hide when she calls
And pretend they're away

If you pass by her grave
You'd best stay with a crowd
For she'll hide in the washing
Disguised as a shroud

Then leap out and give
An affectionate peck
And before you know how
You've two holes in your neck.

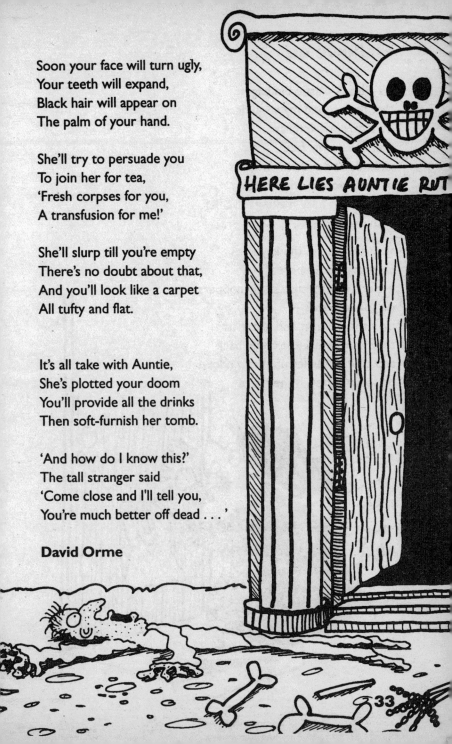

Soon your face will turn ugly,
Your teeth will expand,
Black hair will appear on
The palm of your hand.

She'll try to persuade you
To join her for tea,
'Fresh corpses for you,
A transfusion for me!'

She'll slurp till you're empty
There's no doubt about that,
And you'll look like a carpet
All tufty and flat.

It's all take with Auntie,
She's plotted your doom
You'll provide all the drinks
Then soft-furnish her tomb.

'And how do I know this?'
The tall stranger said
'Come close and I'll tell you,
You're much better off dead . . .'

David Orme

HERE LIES AUNTIE RUT

33

Hallowe'en

it's a black plastic bin bag
that flaps round my shoulders
it's a cardboard mask
that covers my face
and I don't believe in witches
or werewolves or zombies
I'm just out here making mischief
with my mates

shrieking round the keyholes
chanting 'trick or treat' —
a quick way to raise some coppers
or some sweets —
or if they're tight and chase us
they know we'll just come back
and chuck pebbles up the windows
or soapy water in their face

but I don't know why we do it
it's just a laugh:
and I don't believe in witches
like I said
but then I wonder what my mates see
every time they look at me –
do I look as strange as they do
in the dark?

and out there
beyond the streetlamps
and the houselights
and the tellies
where the dark fields slide down
towards the river
can't you feel something waking
something watching
something waiting
something crawling up the alleys
while we clutch each other's hands
and watch the flickering candles
in the withered pumpkin heads
go out like dying stars
as we stand and shiver?

Dave Ward

Have You Ever?

Have you ever . . .
been on a ghost train,
where bats fly,
the shadows sigh
and darkness moans?

Have you ever . . .
heard on a ghost train,
click-clack wheels,
the skeleton squeals
and rattling bones?

Have you ever . . .
seen on a ghost train,
spiders dangle,
cobwebs tangle,
grey tombstones?

Have you ever . . .
felt on a ghost train . . .

NO THANKS!

Judith Nicholls

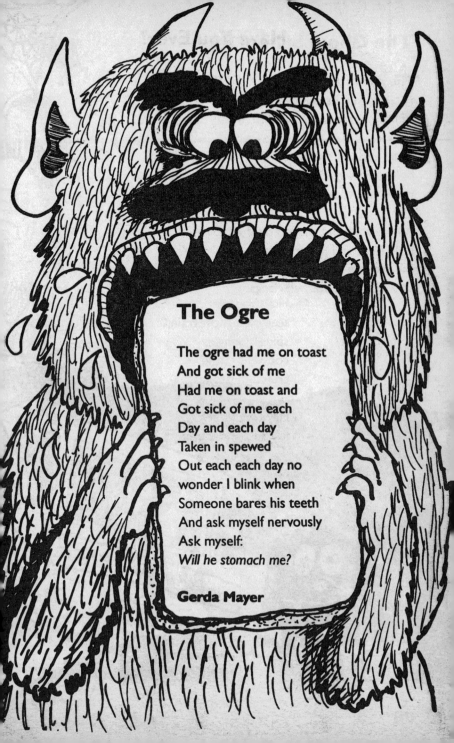

The Ogre

The ogre had me on toast
And got sick of me
Had me on toast and
Got sick of me each
Day and each day
Taken in spewed
Out each each day no
wonder I blink when
Someone bares his teeth
And ask myself nervously
Ask myself:
Will he stomach me?

Gerda Mayer

The Ghoul School Bus

The ghoul school bus
is picking up its cargo
of little horrors.

They must all be home
before first light, when today
turns into tomorrow.

All the sons and daughters of vampires,
little Igors and junior Fangs,
the teenage ghouls with their ghoulfriends
all wail, as the bus bell clangs.

And the driver doesn't look well,
he's robed completely in black,
and the signboard says – 'Transylvania,
by way of hell and back'.

The seats are slimy and wet,
there's a terrible graveyard smell,
all the small ghouls cackle and spit,
and practise their ghoulish spells.

The witches are reading their ABCs,
cackling over 'D' for disease,
while tomboy zombies are falling apart
and werewolves are checking for fleas.

When the bus slows down to drop them off
at Coffin Corner or Cemetery Gates,
their mummies are waiting to greet them
with eyes full of anguish and hate.

The ghoul school bus
is picking up its cargo
of little horrors.

They must all be home
before first light, when today
turns into tomorrow.

Brian Moses

Little

It was a little thing,
such a little thing
and it begged me not to tell.
So I took it by the hand
and it led me into hell.

With almond eyes
– such startled eyes! –
it said it wouldn't hurt.
So I sandalled down the desperate stairs,
slipping on ancient dirt.

With coos and yelps
and triumphant smile
it posted me like a letter.
And here I am as sick as the dead
with no hope of getting better.

It was a little thing,
such a little thing
and it begged me not to tell.
So I took it by the hand
and it led me into hell.

Sue Stewart

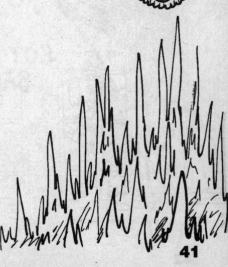

41

On the Late Night Massacre in Putney

Sharp, cold revenge hides silent in the street –
The shadowed werewolf waiting for her prey;
Her jaws gape wide, her tongue hangs graveyard grey,
Her chain-saw teeth drip black with rotten meat.
She'll not forget the three who came and gunned
Her down, and cheered, and left her there for dead;
But werewolves die with silver, not with lead!
Upon the heath she lay long hours, stunned;
But evening shadows healed her scars and she
Soon tasted in the air the gunmen's scent;
Now closer to that dark place come the three
Who, rolling home, tale told, their money spent,
Can have no inkling what their fate will be,
How near those eyes that burn with cold intent.

David Orme

The Quorpzie

Ghost-gibber
ghoul glow,
         that is the gist of
the Quorpzie.

Stench-slobber
stale soul,
         that is the stink of
the Quorpzie.

Groan-gurgler
grunt gob,
         that is the growl of
the Quorpzie.

Skeletoucher
skunk stroke,
         that is the skin of
the Quorpzie.

Clod-cluster
clench kiss,
         that is the clutch of
the Quorpzie.

Mike Johnson

The Spearmint Spuggy from Space Stuck on Every Seat in School

Spuggy on the seat
Chewy on the chair
Bubble gum gunge gets everywhere . . .

It stands on my hands
strands expand like rubber bands.

Congeals and feels like stretch and seal
a scaly skin that you just can't peel.

It smears here inside my ears
and round my eyes . . . bubble gum tears.

Beware! It's there
tangled dreadlocks in my hair.

Look! It's stuck . . .
a pink punk starfish standing up.

It grows all over my nose
so when I breathe a bubble blows

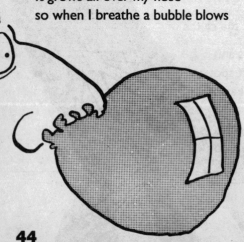

Like polythene or Plasticine
and the bubble that blows is pink and green.

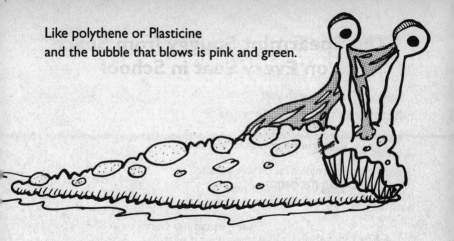

It's pale, a putrid trail
left by a rubber mutant snail
a stringy vest made from the blubber from a whale
a slimy slug with a six-foot tail
syrup stuck on my fingernails.

It clings like strings
of mouldy maggots and horrible things
on the end of my fingers
a big pink wriggly worm it lingers
so that you cannot distinguish
which is the gum and which are my fingers.

Splashes, splodges, blobs and blots,
Blatant blotches, suspect spots,
dabs and dawbs and polka dots
multiplying lots and lots
sticky and strong it has got
the look and feel of alien snot.

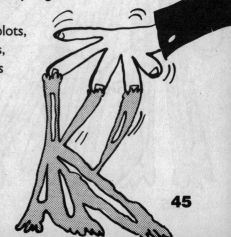

Bleargh! Attishyoo!
This alien is trying to kiss you
it's getting to be an issue
one where you wish you
had more than one Kleenex tissue.

Help! It's drastic
squeezed by snakes of pliable plastic
or an octopus with legs of elastic

Smudges on my shirt
stains on my shoe
a spider's web that's made of glue
I just don't know what to do
with this sticky icky gunged up goo
that pulls so tight my skin turns white
then a nasty shade of blue.
It's true, I haven't got a clue,
what are we going to do?
It's coming for me and it's coming for you . . .

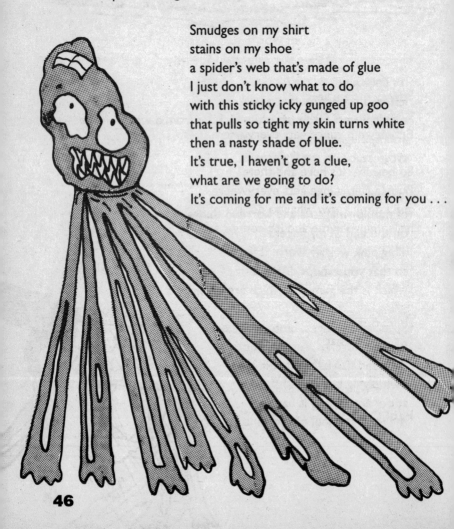

Invasion of the body snatchers
the spuggy on the seats at school will catch us,
plait, matt, attack, attach us.

It's alive and writhes
chokes your throat and blinds your eyes.

Sticks . . . like sick
thick as an oily slick.

Exploding like a can of worms
that slither and slide and slime and squirm.

Spuggy on the seat
Chewy on the chair
Bubble gum gunge gets everywhere.

So beware! It's here and there!
Bubble gum gunge gets everywhere
and I don't know what to do
it's coming for me and it's coming for you
it's coming for me and it's coming for you
Be careful what you chew
Be careful what you chew
it may just get revenge on you
so be careful
        what
            you
                chew . . .

Paul Cookson

It's Only the Storm

'What's that creature that rattles the roof?'
'Hush, it's only the storm.'

'What's blowing the tiles and branches off?'
'Hush, it's only the storm.'

'What's riding the sky like a wild white horse,
Flashing its teeth and stamping its hooves?'

'Hush, my dear, it's only the storm,
Racing the darkness till it catches the dawn.
Hush, my dear, it's only the storm.
When you wake in the morning, it will be gone.'

Dave Ward

Predatory Teacher

He'll wait by the gate for the kid who's late,
His cruel eyes blank as a school roofing slate.
If you felt his pulse, there'd be no heart-rate.
If he had tattoos, well they'd all read: 'HATE!'

You're bound to be found if you clown around
In the corridor, classroom or playground
By this predatory teacher who's renowned
For his creeping round, with hardly a sound.

And he's got weird ears cos he even hears
All your thoughts, ideas and your secret fears.
He's not here. Three cheers! Just then he appears
And he leers and sneers: 'Why, hello, my dears.'

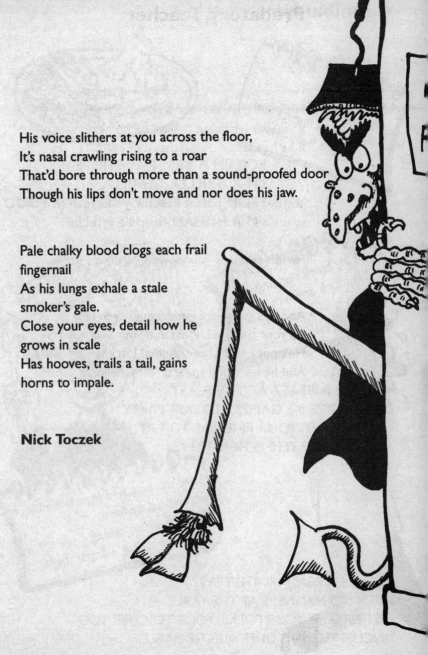

His voice slithers at you across the floor,
It's nasal crawling rising to a roar
That'd bore through more than a sound-proofed door
Though his lips don't move and nor does his jaw.

Pale chalky blood clogs each frail
fingernail
As his lungs exhale a stale
smoker's gale.
Close your eyes, detail how he
grows in scale
Has hooves, trails a tail, gains
horns to impale.

Nick Toczek

Cannibal-isms

Mushy knees
Beans on toes
Fried flesh fingers and
Spaghetti belly-nose.

FOR I'M A BEAST AT THE FEAST
I'M A GRILLER-GORILLA
FROM JUNK FOOD – TO HUNK FOOD
I'M A HUMAN BEAN SWILLER.

Shiny black pudding
Haddock and hips
Toad-in-the-mole
Grilled steak and lips.

'COS I'M A BEAST AT THE FEAST
DON'T GIVE ME GAMES AT YOUR PARTY
I JUST WANT YOUR FRIENDS TO EAT
AND MY APPETITE IS HEARTY!

Give me poached legs, boiled legs
Scrambled or fried.
I'd even eat an omleg
And for pudding – apple thigh.

AND I'M A BEAST AT THE FEAST
WITH NO MANNERS AT THE TABLE
JUST FEED ME YOUR FOLKS, YOUR TEACHER TOO –
UNCLE FRED, MRS DUFF, AUNTIE MABLE.

Jawberries and spineapples
Napericots and plums
Knees and biscuits and
A sticky currant bum.

YES I'M A BEAST AT THE FEAST
IT SEEMS I CAN NEVER GET ENOUGH
I LOVE IRISH STEW – SCOTS AND IRISH TOO
OR A NICE WELSH PEASANT, ROAST AND STUFFED.

Don't get me wrong –
I like a meal with class,
I mean the kind of class
that makes a meal –
Smoked Simon, Colinflower sauce,
A joint of Keith, some nice Jellied Neils,
A hot spicy Kerry, with Margo Chutney,
Brenda Snaps, scrumptious Chop Sue-y,
Bacon and Meg, Minced Pete Tart,
Hot meat and Davey, Jake and Sidney pie,
A leg of Sam, Chocolate Kate,
I adore Pamburgers at a Barbaracue,
Sipping Rasp-Barryade
With your friends – and you.

Grilled nipper
Yorkshire blood
Lancashire tot pot
Head and butter pud.

FOR I'M A BEAST AT THE FEAST
I'LL BE AT YOUR SCHOOL STARTING MONDAY
FOR STEAK AND BUNION, CHEEKS ON TOES
AND LAST OF ALL – EYES SCREAM SUNDAY!

David Horner

Venus Spy Trap

Surreptitiously
he poured
the poisoned wine
into the plant pot.
The plant coughed,
shot out a tendril,
swallowed him,
coughed again
and spat out
his cuff links.

John Desmond

DO-IT-YOURSELF HORROR

AND

THE GAME OF HORROR

DAVID ORME

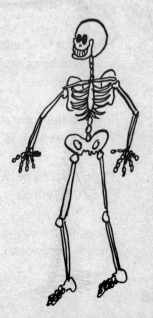

DO-IT-YOURSELF HORROR

Are you a horror fanatic? Do you just love it when those shivers run up and down your back? Are you imaginative enough to be a horror writer yourself? Find out with our **Do-It-Yourself horror checklist!**

At night, do you:

Check under the bed for something nasty before you get in?

Hide your head under the duvet to prevent bits of your face being eaten by the ghouls that lurk behind the wardrobe?

Imagine there are strange creatures in the toilet and rush to get back to bed before the flushing stops?

Hear creaking noises and imagine that SOMEONE or SOMETHING is creeping round your house?

Listen to the sound of the wind and think it's really ghosts, werewolves, or . . . worse?

When you're in the street, do you:

Listen for cars coming along behind you, and run to get round the corner before they go past?

Imagine pillar boxes have eyes?

Hold your breath between lamp posts because the air might be full of poison gas?

Avoid stepping on cracks in case the pavement opens up and you plunge down to a horrible doom?

Avoid walking past certain houses when it's dark?

If you have answered YES to any of these questions, you too could be a horrible poet like the people who have written the poems in this book. You might find some ideas in the checklist to start you off – or try the GAME OF HORROR on page 58.

How to play . . .

The Game of Horror!

YOU WILL NEED:

A Dice

Nerves of Steel

A Group of Horrible Friends

On pages 59, 60 and 61 are three sets of badges of the horrible Creatures, horrible Places and horrible Things you have read about in the poems in this book.

Roll your dice three times; once for a Creature, once for a Place, and once for a Thing. Take it in turns to tell a story with these three elements in it. Dracula's Auntie Ruthless might end up in the crazy bathroom with three million flies, for instance!

Note: One of those little cubes with numbers on is called a die, not a dice, but I thought you had probably had enough horrible words by now!

CREATURES

THE CLASSROOM GHOST

1

CREATURES

WEREWOLF

2

CREATURES

THE QUORZPIE

3

CREATURES

DRACULA'S AUNTIE RUTHLESS

4

CREATURES

THE OGRE

5

CREATURES

PREDATORY TEACHER?

6

59

PLACES

1 UNDER THE FLOORBOARDS

PLACES

2 THE CRAZY BATHROOM

PLACES

3 THE GHOST TRAIN

PLACES

4 THE GHOUL SCHOOL BUS

PLACES

5 STUCK IN A LIFT

PLACES

6 A BLACK SWAMP

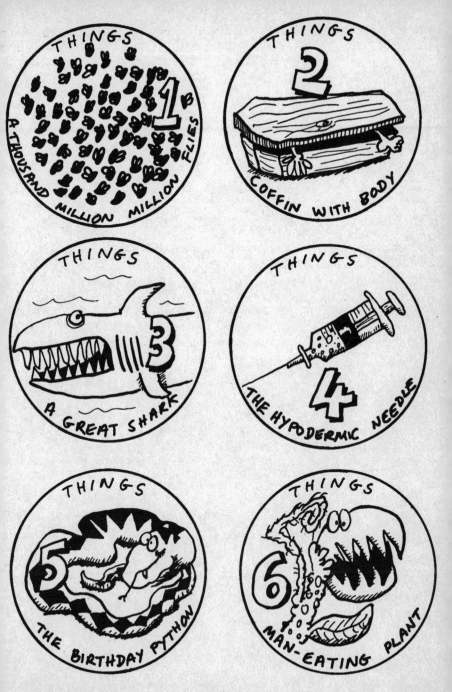

THINGS 1 — A THOUSAND MILLION MILLION FLIES

THINGS 2 — COFFIN WITH BODY

THINGS 3 — A GREAT SHARK

THINGS 4 — THE HYPODERMIC NEEDLE

THINGS 5 — THE BIRTHDAY PYTHON

THINGS 6 — MAN-EATING PLANT